THE ETHICAL PROCESS

A STRATEGY FOR MAKING GOOD DECISIONS

THE ETHICAL PROCESS

▼

A STRATEGY FOR MAKING GOOD DECISIONS

MARVIN T. BROWN, Ph.D.

Prentice Hall
Upper Saddle River, NJ 07458

Library of Congress Cataloging-in-Publication Data
Brown, Marvin T., 1943-
    The ethical process : a strategy for making good decisions / Marvin T. Brown.
        p.   cm.
    ISBN 0-13-397936-9 (pbk.)
    1. Decision-making (Ethics)—Study and teaching.   I. Title.
BJ141.B76   1996   95-36549
170—dc20   CIP

Editorial/Production Supervision,
   Interior Design, and Electronic Paging: *Naomi Sysak*
Managing Editor: *Mary Carnis*
Director of Production: *Bruce Johnson*
Production Coordinator: *Ed O'Dougherty*
Acquisitions Editor: *Elizabeth Sugg*
Editorial Assistant: *Kerry Ribik*
Cover Design: *Wendy Alling-Judy*

Published by Prentice-Hall, Inc.
A Simon & Schuster Company
Upper Saddle River, New Jersey 07458

Printed in the United States of America

10 9 8 7 6 5 4 3 2 1

ISBN 0-13-397936-9

Prentice-Hall International (UK) Limited, *London*
Prentice-Hall of Australia Pty. Limited, *Sydney*
Prentice-Hall Canada Inc., *Toronto*
Prentice-Hall Hispanoamericana, S.A., *Mexico*
Prentice-Hall of India Private Limited, *New Delhi*
Prentice-Hall of Japan, Inc., *Tokyo*
Simon & Schuster Asia Pte. Ltd., *Singapore*
Editora Prentice-Hall do Brasil, Ltda., *Rio de Janeiro*

CONTENTS

▼

CHAPTER THREE

CHAPTER FOUR

APPENDIX

ABOUT THIS WORKBOOK

This workbook is designed for individuals and groups who want to increase their abilities to make good decisions.

You can use it as a supplemental text for various courses—such as business or management courses—that include an ethical analysis of controversial issues. You'll also find its strategy useful for analyzing cases in ethics courses, and the workbook is an ideal manual for ethics training in corporations and other institutions.

For more material on the ethical process, consult my *Working Ethics: Strategies for Decision Making and Organizational Responsibility*. San Francisco, California: Jossey-Bass, 1990.

ACKNOWLEDGMENTS

Special thanks to Eugene Muscat, University of San Francisco, and Sue McKibben, now with the American Hospital Association, for their support at the beginning of this project. I am also grateful to Georges Enderle, University of Notre Dame, Warren A. French, University of Georgia, and Toni Wilson, the Ethics Initiative Manager at Levi Strauss and Company, for helping to improve the workbook, and to Gene Ulansky for his editorial eye.

Marvin T. Brown
Berkeley, California

CHAPTER ONE

THE ETHICAL PROCESS AT WORK

▼

This is a "work" book. Chapter One furnishes the tools and demonstrates how to use them. Chapter Two contains practice sheets. Chapter Three offers different ethical approaches, and Chapter Four unveils a model for using the whole process in seminars and classes.

The Workbook presents ethics as a skill—a skill in making good decisions on controversial issues. This skill relies on our moral response to situations, but it also allows us to move beyond our own response by considering the responses of others. That consideration allows us to work with others to make the best decisions possible.

Decisions are as good as the resources we use to make them. Many poor decisions occur not because decision makers want to make poor decisions, but because they lack important resources. They lack such resources as alternative points of view, relevant information, appropriate values, and other potential courses of action. In many cases, this lack could have been overcome by inviting alternative points of view.

Actually, alternative points of view are already present. Issues are controversial precisely because people have different views about what should be done. Instead of keeping silent about these differences, and therefore not knowing why people highlight some facts and ignore others, this process invites participants to share their positions on issues and then to move into a dialogue that explores the reasons for these positions.

The Ethical Process, then, is a way of working together to make better decisions and fewer mistakes. It is a learning activity. As our groups move through the ethical process, we will learn more than any of us knew before the process started. This increase in knowledge, and in understanding, increases the likelihood that our decision will be the right one.

Q AND A SESSION I.

Q. How will learning to engage in the Ethical Process help the groups I work with?

A. It will enable them to make better decisions and to make fewer mistakes.

Q. How so?

A. Through the Ethical Process groups will discover significant resources that are usually overlooked.

Q. What resources?

A. There are five resources for making decisions:

Five Resources for Making Decisions

Proposals	*Statements about what should be done*
Observations	*Descriptions of what is or is possible*
Value Judgments	*Beliefs about what is important*
Assumptions	*Our taken-for-granted notions of how things work*
Alternative Views	*Other observations, value judgments, and assumptions*

Q. How can we find these resources?

A. Through a process of deliberation and dialogue.

Suppose you are at a meeting where the group must decide what to do. If it is like most meetings, some members already know what they want the group to decide, but they do not all agree. When the group deliberates on different options, speakers rely on different resources. The most significant resources usually remain implicit—and therefore inaccessible—to members of the group.

The Ethical Process can bring these resources to the surface, making them available to all the members.

Q. Will knowing this process foster better decisions?

A. Yes. In each case, some resources will be stronger than others, and the group can select those that let it make the best possible decision.

Q. So, is it fair to say that "Ethics" is a process of making good decisions?

A. Yes. Although some see ethics as already-made decisions—as sets of rules or codes of conduct—these decisions are really the by-products of the ethical process.

    At its core, in other words, ethics is more process than product.

> **The Quality of our**
>
> **Decisions**
>
> **Depends on**
>
> **The Quality of our**
>
> **Resources**

Q. Why do you begin with people taking positions? Usually when meetings begin, participants collect data and share information.

A. Yes, that's true. The question is what information should we collect? As a rule, members of a group collect the information that supports what they want the group to decide. If we begin with participants asserting what they think the group should do, we can better understand the significance of the information.

    Also, by exploring the connection between a position and information, we can begin to ferret out the value judgments and assumptions implicit in that connection.

Q. Are you suggesting that beginning with different proposals can bring the other resources into the deliberation?

A. Yes, our proposals rely on them. The Ethical Process enables us to discover our value judgments and assumptions and to evaluate them.

STARTING POINTS

The Setting:

A group of people must decide how to respond to a controversial issue about which its members disagree.

The Actors:

Persons whose moral responses to issues are based on their feelings, relationships, and beliefs. As moral beings, their senses of right and wrong are rooted in their social, emotional, and cognitive development. Although they disagree with one another on an issue, they do agree to engage in the Ethical Process of investigating the reasons for their different views.

The Action:

A dialogical process enabling participants to work together to discover and then to evaluate the different value judgments and assumptions implicit in their proposals.

The Purpose:

To increase the group's resources—by spelling out its implicit beliefs—so that its members can make the best decision possible.

FOUR RESOURCES FOR DECISION MAKING

Proposals

- Prescriptive statements—suggest actions.
- Rely on observations, value judgments, and assumptions.
- Can be evaluated by examining supporting reasons.

Observations

- Descriptive statements—describe situations.
- Rely on correct presentation of the "facts."
- Usually can be verified through more research.
- Can be evaluated by degree of objectivity.

Value Judgments

- Normative statements—guide actions.
- Rely on assumptions.
- Make the connection between proposal and observation.
- Cannot be verified by empirical research.
- Can be evaluated by different ethical traditions.

Assumptions

- Reflective statements—express world views and attitudes.
- Rely on culture, religion, social, and personal history.
- Usually taken for granted, but may be found in theories.
- Can be evaluated by such criteria as relevance, consistency, and inclusiveness.

SORTING OUT THE DIFFERENT RESOURCES

Identify the following statements as proposals (P), observations (O), value judgments (VJ), or assumptions (A).

1. _____ We should develop a child care center for our company.

2. _____ A growing number of people in the workfore have parental responsibilities.

3. _____ We have an obligation to consider employee needs.

4. _____ Work and family life strongly affect one another.

5. _____ We should be fair.

6. _____ Give people an inch, they will take a mile.

7. _____ Some US companies moved to Mexico to avoid environmental regulations.

8. _____ We should do what produces the most good and the least harm.

9. _____ Discrimination against women and people of color continues to be practiced today.

10. _____ All people should have some opportunities for fulfilling their life plans.

---

1. P   2. O   3. VJ   4. A   5. VJ   6. A   7. O   8. VJ   9. O   10. VJ

DIFFERENCES AMONG THE FOUR RESOURCES

Proposals are answers to questions. Good questions generate good proposals. The best questions are specific and action-oriented. "Should we do X?" Proposals are specific should statements that answer such questions.

Value judgments can also be asserted as "should statements," or translated into them. Unlike proposals, value judgments are general statements. Compare item 1 on page 6, for example, to items 3, 5, and 10. The latter do not say precisely what should be done, but rather offer general guidelines for action.

A statement qualifies as an observation if contrary evidence can disprove it. Item 2, for example, could be refuted by contrary evidence. Item 3, a value judgment, could not.

Some observations include concepts that need defining. Even though definitions are kinds of assumptions, once you have defined a term, you can then use it to make observations. If you define freedom as the capacity for self-development, for example, then you could observe that some condition limits your freedom because it limits your capacity for self-development.

Observations sometimes look like assumptions. They both appear to describe. A key difference is that observations are usually specific and are subject to empirical evidence. Note items 2, 7, and 9 on page 6. Assumptions are general. Item 6 is an example. The following chart summarizes the key differences among the four resources.

	Action-Orientation	Descriptive-Orientation
Specific	**Proposals**	**Observations**
General	**Value Judgments**	**Assumptions**

ALTERNATIVE VIEWS
The Fifth Resource

INITIATE THE ETHICAL PROCESS

PROVIDE ANOTHER SET OF RESOURCES: PROPOSALS, OBSERVATIONS, VALUE JUDGMENTS, AND ASSUMPTIONS

GIVE VOICE TO DIFFERENT ASPIRATIONS

MAY PREVENT MISTAKES

Some groups welcome alternative views, since they offer so many benefits, but such openness is not always the case. Our acceptance of alternative views depends on how we feel about disagreement. Consider these possible advantages and disadvantages:

Advantages of Disagreement	Disadvantages of Disagreement
Allows us to examine reasons	Threatens cooperation
Increases the pool of resources	Creates a debating game of winners and losers
Reveals a proposal's limits	
Promotes a more inclusive and realistic proposal	Favors "argumentative"types over others
Creates opportunity for learning	Stifles participation

If you look closely, the advantages column refers to issues and decisions, and the disadvantages column to persons and relations. Many people equate disagreement with an attack on a person. To benefit from the advantages and to minimize the possible disadvantages, groups will need to acknowledge the relational aspects of disagreement while "agreeing" to focus on reasons, not on the persons expressing them.

Your group will need to develop a cooperative spirit. A good way to begin is by working together to discover the reasons for different views. Whether this cooperation can happen depends on how the members "face" disagreements.

FACING DISAGREEMENTS

Determine which of the following statements seem true, which seem false, and share your answers with others.

1. ___ Most people do what they think is right considering the world they think they live in.

2. ___ Reasons should be evaluated on their merit, not on who expresses them.

3. ___ If people disagree with me, it's probably because they don't understand me.

4. ___ Disagreeing with a proposal does not mean disagreeing with all the reasons that support it.

5. ___ We learn more from people who disagree with us than from people who agree with us.

6. ___ Some differences need not lead to disagreements.

7. ___ If people ignore their disagreements, they will usually become more productive.

8. ___ People will usually not express their disagreements unless they believe others will listen and respond.

9. ___ Many mistakes occur because people refuse to listen to other views.

10. ___ Most disagreements occur in the context of broader agreements.

GATHERING RESOURCES

Disagreement is not only a fact of everyday life, it is also the source for different observations, value judgments, and assumptions.

These resources, however, do not exist alone. They are embedded in the experiences and beliefs of specific groups. If all the concerned groups are not somehow represented in a decision making process, that process remains incomplete, and the decisions fragile.

List the groups that should be included in discussions of the following issues so that the decision makers will have the advantage of all significant resources.

Downsizing _____

Corporate responsibility _____

Public education reform _____

Executive pay _____

Health care reform _____

Computerization of the workplace _____

Affirmative action _____

Parental leave _____

Cultural diversity programs_____

Environmental regulation_____

A BACKGROUND NOTE

The "ethical process" belongs to a long tradition of discourse—the practice of thinking and talking together. Its classical roots come from Aristotle's development of the practical syllogism in his *Nicomachean Ethics* and the enthymeme in his *Rhetoric*.

The practical syllogism consists of two kinds of premises or reasons: universal and particular. By relating them, one can draw a conclusion about what to do. "Vegetables are good for all persons. I am a person. Therefore, vegetables are good for me."

The enthymeme is a practical syllogism with one unspoken premise. Aristotle advises public speakers to learn the beliefs of their audience, and then to rely on them in recommending action. The beliefs function as universal or general principles that connect observations with actions. Since the audience already possesses these beliefs, it is not necessary to voice them.

A second major contribution to this tradition was made by the British philosopher, David Hume (1711-1776), who argued that there is no necessary connection between "what is" and "what ought to be." The move from description to prescription, in other words, always involves a third element, a normative premise, which we call a "value judgment."

Although we continually rely on normative beliefs or general "should" premises, when making observations to support our proposals, we only need to consider them when people disagree with us—when they do not rely on the same value judgments.

More recently, Stephen Toulmin in *The Uses of Argument* (1957), outlined an argumentative form that showed how the general premise (or value judgment) that connects action and data relies on its own backing, or what we have called practical assumptions. Toulmin also developed the notion of qualifying one's conclusions.

This tradition has shown that our thinking and talking rely on a variety of resources. Some of the most significant usually remain hidden—at first.

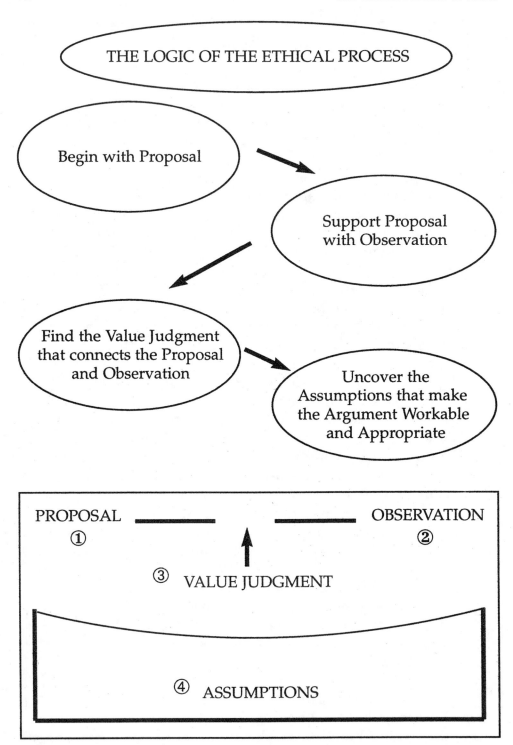

HOW THE RESOURCES WORK TOGETHER

Proposal   States what should   *We should provide*
                        be done.   *universal health*
                                                  coverage.

Observation   Provides relevant   *(Because) people who*
                        "facts" to support   *cannot afford*
                        the proposal.   *coverage do not*
                                                  receive adequate care.

Value Judgment   Fills the gap   *When we are able to*
                        between the pre-   *provide care, we*
                        scriptive proposal   *should provide it for*
                        and the descriptive   *all.*
                        observation.

Assumption   Cradles the whole   *We are all part of an*
                        argument in a   *interdependent health*
                        worldview.   *care system. Health*
                                                  care is a necessary
                                                  condition for self-
                                                  fulfillment.

Alternative Views   Makes additional   *Why not keep the sys-*
                        resources available.   *tem we have?*

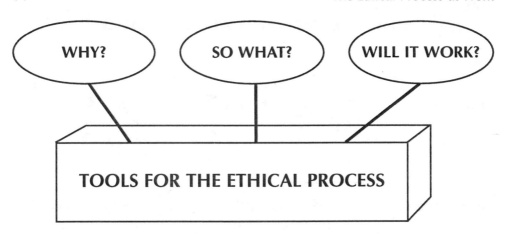

After stating a proposal, the question **"WHY?"** asks for some evidence (an observation) to support it. Observations describe. Descriptive sentences, however, cannot justify prescriptive statements. What *is* does not tell us what *should be*. The question **"SO WHAT?"** exposes the gap between the proposal and the observation, and thereby elicits the implicit value judgment. The question **"WILL IT WORK?"** asks for our taken for granted notions of how things work—our pragmatic assumptions.

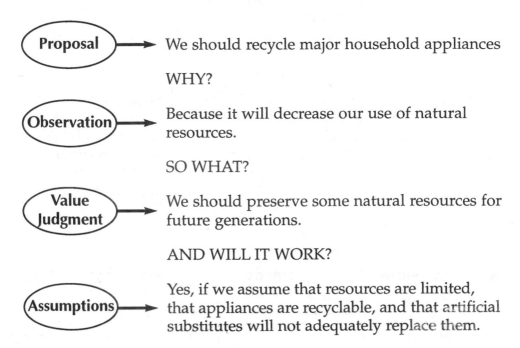

IMPLICIT PREMISES

Find the implicit premise of the following arguments and identify them as observations or value judgments.

We should listen to what Jose has to say because our decision will seriously affect him.

We should decrease taxes because the people do not want an increase.

We should limit the amount of money allowed in political campaigns because now only the wealthy can run for national office.

We should not allow people to decide when to die because they may make a mistake.

We should increase everyone's wages because profits have increased.

We should share information because we should respect one another.

We should share some of our abundance with the hungry because hunger is painful.

HOW TO UNCOVER VALUE JUDGMENTS

("Value judgment," "normative statement," and "implicit principle" are used interchangeably here.)

1. Select the key terms of the proposal and the observation, and use them to develop a normative statement—a statement that guides our actions.

    Proposal: We should *reward* everyone on the team,

    Observation: because the team members *worked together.*

    Value Judgment: ALL WHO WORKED TOGETHER SHOULD BE REWARDED.

2. Rewrite the observation as a normative statement.

    Proposal: We should increase our training program for those who work with toxic chemicals,

    Observation: because it will increase worker safety.

    Value Judgment: WE SHOULD MAINTAIN A SAFE WORK PLACE.

3. Formulate the Implicit Principle in the Proposal.

    Proposal: We should tell Wanda her position is being phased out,

    Observation: because she inquired about our plans.

    Value Judgment: PEOPLE HAVE A RIGHT TO KNOW DECISIONS ABOUT THEIR FUTURE. or, WE SHOULD TELL THE TRUTH.

HOW TO UNCOVER ASSUMPTIONS

Many assumptions are taken for granted. We are unaware of them. Paradoxically, sometimes we can see other's assumptions much better than we can see our own. By working together, we can help each other gain an understanding of our assumptions. The following graph shows how it works. Carol first imagines Maria's assumptions. She then uses these assumptions as a mirror to uncover her own.

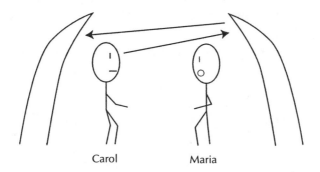

Carol   Maria

Carol could imagine: "What assumptions might Maria have?" "Since I do not have those assumptions, what assumptions might I have?"

A second way to uncover assumptions is to imagine a "different world" that may not exist, but if it did, you would change your mind. It may help to use If-Then statements.

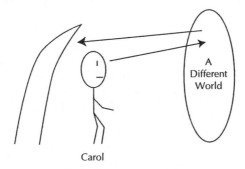

Carol

Carol could say in this case: "If the world were 'such and such,' then I would change my mind." "Since I am not assuming such a world, what kind of world am I assuming?"

HOW TO USE ALTERNATIVE VIEWS

1. Exploring alternative views offers more resources for making decisions.

   Although alternative views "oppose" your proposal, when you begin to uncover the reasons that support their position, you will find that many of their observations, value judgments, and assumptions are not "opposed" to yours, but rather merely different. They may see things that you did not notice. By exploring what their positions rely on, you increase your group's resources for making decisions.

2. The alternative view can help you understand your assumptions.

   Examine the assumptions the alternative view relies on. Ask how the assumptions of your view differ from the assumptions of the alternative view. For example, you may argue for a wage increase because of increased living costs. The alternative view argues against the increase because of decreasing profit. The alternative view may assume that wages should be tied to profitability. If your position does not share this assumption, on what contrasting assumption does it rely? Perhaps that wages should be tied to household expenses.

3. The alternative view can help improve your proposal.

   In the example above, the alternative view's "best reason" for not increasing wages may be that the company's profit margin has been decreasing. This explanation may count as a "good reason" that you should take into account. Instead of arguing for a wage increase at all costs, the good reason of the alternative view can help you see the limits of your proposal. You could include it in a modified proposal: "The company should increase wages unless the increase thrusts the company into financial difficulties."

IDENTIFY THE PARTS OF THE ETHICAL PROCESS IN THE FOLLOWING EXAMPLE, AND EXPLAIN HOW THEY WERE DEVELOPED.

Should Joan leave the company for a better job or stay for six months and help her team finish its project?

Joan should stay.

Joan should not stay.

Because the team members have agreed to work together on this projet.

Because the new job provides new opportunities for her career development.

People should keep their promises.

People should increase their competence and develop their potential.

The alternative view may assume that she cannot develop her potential here, so I must assume that she can.

The first view must assume that group solidarity is more important than individual development, so I must assume the opposite.

Joan should stay if there are opportunities for learning and developing competencies.

Joan should not stay if her leaving prevents the team from accomplishing its goals.

(Joan decides to leave because the team cannot imagine how to change Joan's work to give her more learning opportunities and it appears that the team can find someone else to do her work.)

SOME INFERENCES FROM CHAPTER ONE

THE QUALITY OF OUR DECISIONS DEPENDS ON THE
QUALITY OF OUR RESOURCES.

NO ONE HAS ALL THE GOOD RESOURCES.

THE INCREASE IN RESOURCES USUALLY BEGINS
WITH DISAGREEMENT.

WHEN PEOPLE DISAGREE ABOUT WHAT TO DO,
THEY PROVIDE AN OCCASION FOR INVESTIGATING
THE REASONS FOR DIFFERENT VIEWS.

SUCH AN INVESTIGATION CAN UNCOVER
OBSERVATIONS, VALUE JUDGMENTS, AND ASSUMP-
TIONS THAT WILL GIVE INDIVIDUALS AND GROUPS
MORE RESOURCES THAN THEY HAD BEFORE.

THE ABUNDANCE OF RESOURCES CAN OVERCOME
A WIN/LOSE MENTALITY THAT DISAGREEMENT
TOO EASILY AROUSES, AND IT CAN PROVIDE FOR A
SHARING WHERE EVERYONE BENEFITS.

ALTHOUGH HAVING MORE RESOURCES DOES NOT
ALWAYS MEAN THE END OF DISAGREEMENT, IT
DOES ASSURE EVERYONE THAT THE DECISION
RESTS UPON A CONSIDERATION OF THE BEST
RESOURCES AVAILABLE.

YOUR COMMENTS AND QUESTIONS

Write below your comments and questions about the ethical process. Your class or group should take some time to share each other's concerns.

_____

_____

_____

_____

_____

_____

_____

_____

_____

_____

_____

_____

_____

_____

_____

CHAPTER TWO

WORKSHEETS FOR ENGAGING IN THE ETHICAL PROCESS

▼

The following worksheets guide you through a process of developing—in the sense of unfolding—and evaluating the five resources for making decisions.

As you move through the process, you will probably find some reasons on different sides of an issue that you favor and some you disagree with. You will also be able to pinpoint the source of the disagreement between the two proposals. By sorting out the strong and weak reasons, you may discover a new proposal– one that relies on the strengths of both views.

A reason's strength depends on what kind it is. Observations, value judgments, and assumptions all have their own criteria. Some of these criteria have been provided on the appropriate worksheets, and you may supply others from your own resources.

As you move through the process, you will find some agreements that may facilitate a new proposal. If this is not possible, you can use the alternative view's strengths to qualify your own position. Qualifying your position means that you use the best reasons of the alternative view to set some limits on the implementation of your proposal.

These worksheets allow you to focus on different agreements and disagreements, rather than on persons agreeing and disagreeing. Since your task is to develop both pro and con arguments, you will "face" yourself rather than someone else.

WORKSHEET # 1

Formulating the Question

Sometimes, people disagree about what needs to be addressed. The question of universal health care coverage, for example, may be taken as a question about government's role in providing services, or about individual responsibility. In many cases, clarification of the "real" question will save a lot of time as well as prevent misunderstanding. Many issues, of course, raise a series of questions. In such cases, we need to agree how to proceed through the series, so all of us address the same question at the same time.

To ensure a fair dialogue, you need to make sure all parties accept how the question is formulated. If you are not sure of your formulation, you can ask whether other interested groups might formulate it differently.

Describe a situation or controversial issue that needs to be addressed.

_____

_____

_____

Would others describe it differently? If so, how?

_____

_____

_____

Formulate the question about what should be done as fairly as possible.

What should we do about _____

_____

_____

WORKSHEET # 2

Your View

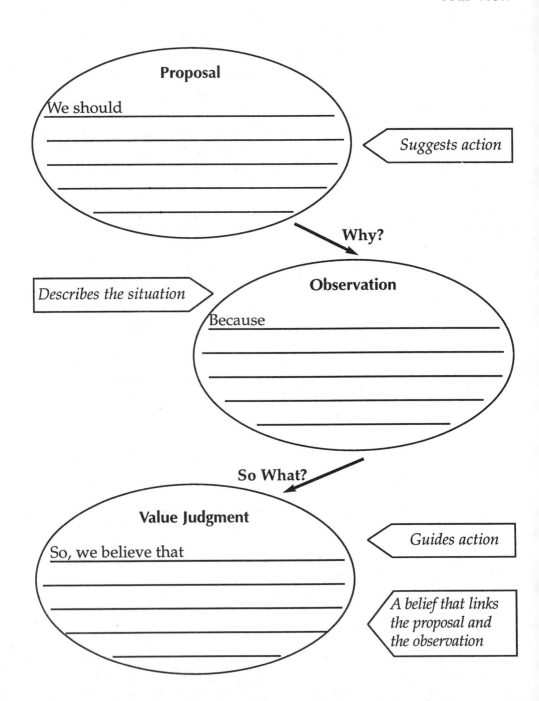

WORKSHEET # 3

Alternative View

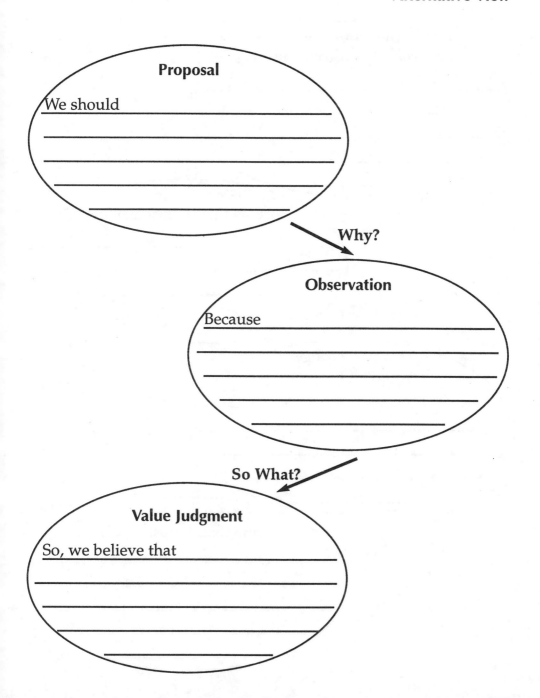

Proposal

We should _____

_____

_____

_____

Why?

Observation

Because _____

_____

_____

_____

_____

So What?

Value Judgment

So, we believe that _____

_____

_____

_____

WORKSHEET # 4

Use Different Assumptions to Discover Your Own

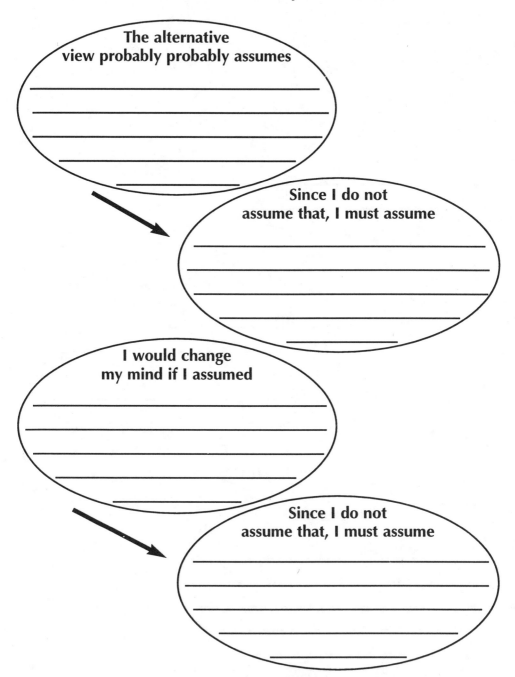

WORKSHEET # 5

Evaluate Observations

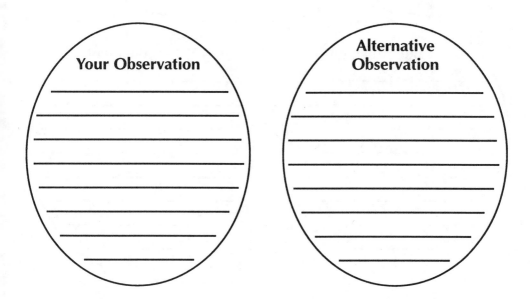

Evaluation:

- Are both observations descriptive sentences that can be supported by evidence?

- If they are different, do they also oppose one another?

- Can both observations be true?

- How might others rewrite the observations?

- Are these observations the source of the disagreement between the two views?

If both parties acknowledge the truth of each other's observation, they can see places where they agree even though they disagree about what should be done. This is a common experience and demonstrates that the ethical process can develop agreements as it explores disagreements. If the different observations do not conflict with one another, then the disagreement probably resides in different value judgments or assumptions.

WORKSHEET # 6

Evaluate Value Judgments

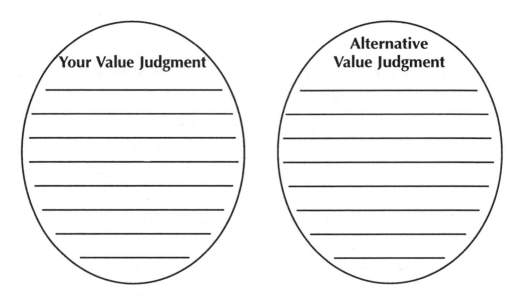

Your Value Judgment

Alternative Value Judgment

Evaluation:

- Does each value judgment clearly connect the proposal and observation? If not, rewrite them so they do.

- Are they normative statements, i.e. statements that express standards of conduct or values?

- Could you affirm both value judgments if they were standing alone?

- Are the value judgments the source of the disagreement between the two views?

- Would one value judgment usually override the other?

- What do you think is the source of these different value judgments?

If the disagreement resides at the level of value judgments, you can use the ethical theories presented in the next Chapter to evaluate them. These theories may also generate more resources for making the best decision possible.

WORKSHEET # 7

Evaluate Assumptions

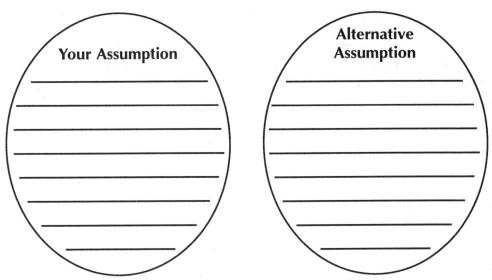

Evaluation:

- Are the assumptions contradictory or only different?
- If merely different, are there other assumptions or value judgments that explain the disagreement?
- Are these assumptions grounded in cultural, religious, social, or gender differences?
- If contradictory, is this contradiction the source of the disagreement?
- Can one assumption function as the context for the other (such as cooperation is the context for competition)?
- Are there theories that have explored these assumptions?
- Are there broader assumptions or value judgments that may serve as a container for this disagreement?

Once you have discovered the source of the disagreement, you can evaluate its significance for the group and its task. Sometimes people can agree to disagree and still cooperate in common endeavors. Whether this is possible depends on the strength of the agreements.

WORKSHEET # 8

Working with Agreements

After evaluating all the resources, you may have found some observations, value judgments, and assumptions that you would accept if they were standing alone rather than as part of an alternative view. If we separate them from the argument, we can usually find significant agreements. State the important agreements you have discovered.

Agreements

_____

_____

_____

_____

_____

These agreements may serve:

1. As a basis for envisioning new proposals that include the most important value judgments and/or assumptions.

2. As leverage to negotiate a compromise.

3. As acknowledgment of a common ground.

If possible, write a new proposal that relies on agreements. If not possible, move to the next worksheet.

_____

_____

WORKSHEET # 9

Working with Disagreements

Write below what you see as the best reason—observation, value judgment, or assumption—of each argument.

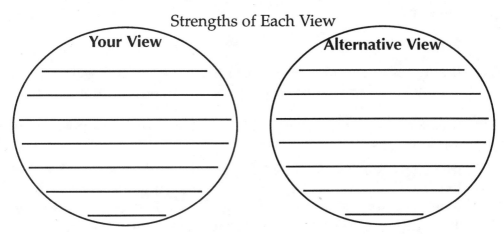

Strengths of Each View

Your View

Alternative View

Use each strength as a possible qualification of the proposals. Qualifications help us understand the limits of our good ideas. For example, some may argue against their company providing child care because it costs too much money. Someone arguing for child care could use this reason to monitor the development of a child care center (e.g., "We should make full-time child care available to all our employees *unless* that exceeds our budget"). If it did cost more than we had thought, then the qualification could prevent a good proposal from turning into a bad practice.

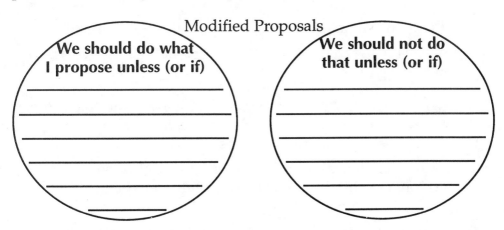

Modified Proposals

We should do what I propose unless (or if)

We should not do that unless (or if)

Q AND A SESSION II.

Q. So, you think we should use this process at work?

A. Yes, the process will enable people to make better decisions and fewer mistakes.

Q. Is that an assumption?

A. It may rest on assumptions, but I think we can find evidence to support this statement, which makes it an observation.

Q. If observations are supported by evidence, what supports your assumptions?

A. In a sense, our assumptions support everything else. They are the foundation on which we build our arguments. We can evaluate them, however, by such criteria as relevance, consistency, and unity. For example, if an argument assumes that individuals exist alone and yet we know that we always live in and out of relationships, then we can notice that the assumption is inconsistent and needs some revision. In some cases, of course, theoretical studies can help us understand our assumptions, such as studies about human nature.

Q. I see. Let's say I agree with your observation that this process will improve our decisions. So what?

A. So, I believe we should make the best decisions we can.

Q. Is that your value judgment?

A. Yes. It's a belief that connects the observation and proposal. Do you agree with it?

Q. Yes. It seems we share similar values. I understand the different kinds of statements now, but do you really think knowing this will help us make better decisions?

A. The answer depends on our assumptions. Let me ask you a question. Do you think nutritional studies are helpful?

Q. Yes. Such studies allow us to select healthy foods instead of just eating whatever appears before us. If you want to be healthy, they certainly are helpful.

A. Exactly. Likewise, becoming conscious of the values and assumptions on which we rely will also be worth the effort for people who want to make better decisions.

Q. I see your point. How would you fit the statement you just made about the similarity between understanding the resources for making decisions and nutritional studies into the argumentative framework?

A. We call this an argument by analogy. It relies on a similarity between eating and decision making. Since the analogy involves descriptive rather than normative statements, it belongs to the observation-assumption column on page 7. The similarities can be observed. Their significance depends on our assumptions.

Q. And what was the purpose of the analogy?

A. To support the assumption that becoming conscious of the resources on which we rely will improve our decisions. An alternative view might have a different assumption, such as the best decisions are intuitive or spontaneous. Since I do not hold that assumption, I must assume that the best decisions are thoughtful and thought-out. The alternative assumption does have some merit, but in a group process where people disagree, it seems that a thoughtful process will be more appropriate.

Q. I guess I forgot about the element of disagreement.

A. An important element. If everyone agrees, the decision making process will remain mostly unconscious. It's only when people disagree that a group has the opportunity to gather and then to evaluate its resources.

Q. How can they evaluate their resources?

A. I'm glad you asked. That is the subject of the next chapter.

YOUR COMMENTS AND QUESTIONS

Write below your comments and questions about discovering different resources—observations, value judgments, and assumptions—by
working with alternative views.

_____

_____

_____

_____

_____

_____

_____

_____

_____

_____

_____

_____

_____

_____

_____

_____

_____

CHAPTER THREE

EVALUATING ARGUMENTS FROM DIFFERENT ETHICAL APPROACHES

▼

In the process of discovering different observations, value judgments, and assumptions, we like to think that some are stronger than others. How can we tell? One way is to see how they fare when measured by different ethical traditions.

This chapter presents three traditions or ethical approaches that together provide a set of criteria for looking at the strengths of different views : teleology, deontology, and utilitarianism. Each of these three—the first of which we'll call an ethics of purpose, the second an ethics of principle, and the third an ethics of consequence—has its own approach.

AN ETHICS OF PURPOSE focuses on the "telos"—the final end or purpose—of the agent. An agent decides what should be done. The agent's "end" is the good for which he or she strives. Proposals that help to achieve that good are right; those that hinder it are wrong.

AN ETHICS OF PRINCIPLE focuses on the implicit principle in a proposal, and sees if it can be willed as a universal moral law. It also looks at whether the proposal shows respect for others.

AN ETHICS OF CONSEQUENCE focuses on the positive and negative effects a proposal will have on the people affected.

Whereas an ethics of purpose looks at whether an act will bring about the agent's purpose, an ethics of consequence looks at the act's consequences upon everyone affected. (Acts have consequences, not purposes. Agents have purposes, not consequences.)

Select a controversial issue, develop alternative arguments on the following two worksheets, and then use the three ethical approaches' worksheets to evaluate them.

**Select a controversial issue and
develop the four resources**

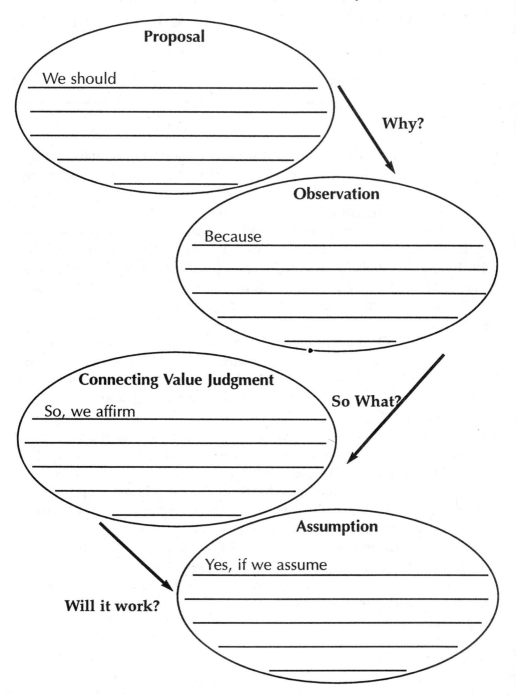

**Develop the resources of
an Alternative view**

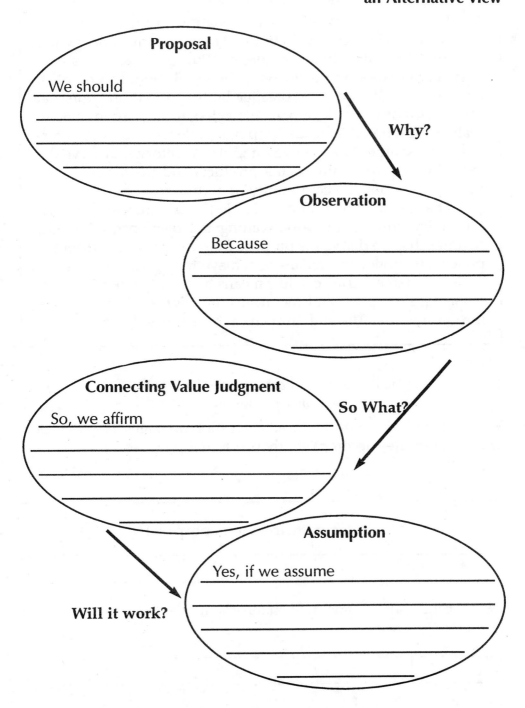

AN ETHICS OF PURPOSE

An ethics of purpose begins by formulating an agent's purpose. The agent can be either an individual or an organization—whoever decides what should be done. "Purpose" functions as a normative term—expressing what the agent should accomplish and become. It's best to consider both external and internal purposes. For example, a person's external purpose may be to realize one's potential or develop one's talents, and one's internal purpose might be to have integrity. A factory may have the external purpose of producing products and the internal purpose of developing a community of mutual respect.

The trick here is to not scramble the relationship between the policy and the purpose. Getting the relationship straight requires that we derive the purpose from the agent, not from the policy. The policy is a means to achieve the agent's purpose or end. Ends have intrinsic value; means have instrumental value. If the ends are good and the means are aligned with them the means are right. The end, in such cases, justifies the means.

*You apply this ethical approach by beginning
with the agents.*

Who are the agents addressing the question on pages 34 and 35 and what should they accomplish (their external purpose)?

_____

_____

What should they become (their internal purpose)?

_____

_____

Which proposals (means) will enable them to achieve these purposes (ends)?

_____

_____

AN ETHICS OF PRINCIPLE

An ethics of principle first looks for the implicit principle in the policy statement. The implicit principle is a general, normative statement that can be derived from the specific, prescriptive policy. This approach then tests the implicit principle with the principle of universality. "Can you will that the implicit principle become a universal law?" This universality is based on consistency, not consensus.

If the implicit principle involves breaking a promise, for example, it would be impossible to will that everyone should obey it, because no one would make promises if people had a duty to break them. One could not rationally (consistently) accept a world, in other words, where everyone broke their promises.

Since persons decide what counts as a moral law through their own rational will, they deserve respect. They should be treated as moral agents—persons who exercise their freedom in willing what laws should be obeyed. Therefore, a policy must respect the moral agency of others.

You apply this ethical approach by beginning with the proposal.

What are the implicit principles of the proposals on pages 34 and 35?

_____

_____

Can we will that these principles become universal rules that apply in all such cases?

_____

_____

Do the proposals respect the moral agency of others?

_____

_____

IN SOME PROPOSALS, THE IMPLICIT PRINCIPLE IDENTIFIES VARIOUS NOTIONS OF JUSTICE AND RIGHTS.

To evaluate these principles, we can ask three questions: (1) What is being distributed? (2) What would be a just distribution? and (3) What rights follow from this type of distribution?

(1) **"What is being distributed?"** asks about the goods or things that some people receive for some reason. They may range from recognition to money to pain.

(2) **"What would be a just distribution?"** selects the type of justice that seems to "fit" with the good being distributed. For example, public education should be distributed by membership, while bonuses should be distributed by contribution. The following criteria for justice include most of the ways we distribute things:

Need	Those who need more receive more.
Membership	All members receive equally.
Contribution	Those who give more, receive more.
Merit	Those with special talents or status receive more.
Choice	People get what they choose.

(3) **"What rights follow from this type of distribution?"** enables us to discover the rights people have when things are distributed justly. Three kinds of rights are

Human rights	Claims to goods that should be distributed to everyone, such as the right to subsistence.
Civic rights	Claims to goods that should be distributed to all citizens, such as the right to vote.
Contractual rights	Claims to goods that we have agreed to distribute in a specific way, such as wages or benefits.

"What is just?" or "What rights should be acknowledged?" are controversial questions. Their answers lie mainly in our assumptions about the meaning of things (goods). Discussions about these assumptions can sometimes resolve the controversy.

Using the chart below, list the significant goods distributed in the controversy on page 34 and 35. Then select the appropriate type of justice for each good. Most goods should be distributed according to need, membership, contribution, merit, or choice. Finally, select what individual right—human, civic, or contractual—corresponds to the type of justice you have chosen. In some cases, you may find it easier to first assign the individual right and then select the type of justice that belongs to it.

Goods Distributed	Types of Justice	Individual Rights

If you are unsure about how specific goods should be distributed, you can list them below and examine different assumptions about their meaning today. See if some assumptions are more consistent and universal than others.

_____

_____

_____

_____

_____

_____

AN ETHICS OF CONSEQUENCES

An ethics of consequence examines the consequences of different proposals on the various groups affected by a decision, and recommends the proposal that produces more positive and fewer negative consequences. In contrast to an ethics of purpose's focus on the agent's purpose, this approach looks at an act's consequences.

This approach always faces the difficulty of measuring and comparing very different consequences. The measurements will become more reliable if all of the groups affected by the consequences have a voice in their interpretation.

Sometimes it is important to balance short-term and long-term consquences or to include future generations.

You can apply this approach by beginning with the proposal's effects on different groups.

What groups will be affected by the decision on the issue explored on pages 34 and 35?

_____

_____

What will be the positive and negative consequences of each proposal for these groups?

_____

_____

Which proposal has the most positive and least negative consequences?

_____

_____

If all three approaches support a proposal or facilitate a new proposal, then your argument may be very sound. If only some of the approaches support your argument, then you may want to develop other purposes, principles, and consequences, and at the same time, to experiment with other options, since the strongest argument will have the support of all three approaches.

THE ETHICAL APPROACHES AND THE RESOURCES
FOR MAKING DECISIONS

	Observations	Value Judgment	Assumption
Purpose	The function, potential, or nature of the agent	The good purposes that the agent should strive to achieve	The agent's good purposes provide the criteria for evaluating acts
Principle	Implicit maxim or principle of a proposal	Universal, consistent moral laws and respect for a person's moral agency	Persons achieve dignity through willing consistent moral principles
Consequence	Probable positive and negative consequences of different proposals	Most positive and least negative consequences for all affected by the proposals	Capacity to know and to measure consequences for different groups.

ETHICS OF PURPOSE: *We should test the safety of our products (P) because that will insure quality products (O), which should be one of our purposes (VJ) as a business (A).*

ETHICS OF PRINCIPLE: *We should test the safety of our products (P) because this proposal implies that people should exercise due care toward others (O), which can be willed as a universal law (VJ) by moral agents (A).*

ETHICS OF CONSEQUENCE: *We should test the safety of our products (P) because this proposal produces more positive and less negative consequences than other proposals (O), and we should do what has the better overall consequences for all involved (VJ), assuming our projections are correct (A).*

Q AND A SESSION III.

Q. Can you really observe the "function, potential, or nature of an agent" as the chart of the previous page says?

A. Suppose a group at a medical center considers whether to train its employees in the ethical process. From an ethics of purpose approach, it would begin by thinking about its identity. What kind of place is it? People could probably agree that it is a health center empowered by people with different types of training and abilities. This answer would be an "observation." They could also observe how it currently fits in with other health services and the general health care system. Such an analysis would describe what we could call "the function, potential, or nature of an agent."

Q. OK. Then how do you get from this descriptive work to the purpose?

A. Basically, you get there by relying on assumptions. Some people may assume that the purpose of health centers should be limited to promoting physical health, while others may assume that the centers should have a broader purpose, including even the promotion of spiritual health. The "good" purpose arises out of the discussion between observations and assumptions. The key assumption, however, is that the medical center does have a "good" purpose that it should strive to achieve. If training in the ethical process helps to achieve it, then it would be justified.

Q. Where does this way of thinking come from?

A. From Aristotle, the Greek philosopher, who is usually given credit for establishing ethics as a discipline.

Q. Cool. And the ethics of principle?

A. From Immanuel Kant, an eighteenth-century German philosopher. You can also find traces of early Jewish and Christian ethics in this approach, such as the Golden Rule.

Q. And what does one observe in this approach?

A. The ethics of principle doesn't directly take into account the particularities of a situation. It does "look at" the implicit principle of any proposal, so this could be called an observation. It is the only descriptive work in this approach.

Q.   But it is stretching it a bit to call that an observation.

A.   A bit. It's an imperfect world.

Q.   So it is. How would you tackle the question of training from an ethics of principle approach?

A.   First I would "observe" the implicit principle, or maybe I should say that I first construct it and then "see" if it really fits the proposal. What about this: "People should receive the training they need to do their jobs?" That "looks" like a possible implicit principle. Can we will that it become a universal moral rule? I think so. It affirms that there should be some congruence or consistency between skills and job requirements. Not to provide training, but to demand good decisions, would be inconsistent or contradictory. You could not will that as a universal moral law.

Q.   I get it. The third approach, an ethics of consequence, seems the easiest. Who developed this approach?

A.   Two British philosophers, Jeremy Bentham and John Stuart Mill. It may look easier because this approach appears to rely more on observations than the other two. As you begin comparing different possible consequences, however, it can become overwhelming, especially when people disagree about the meaning or value of different consequences. In such cases, the other two approaches can complement an ethics of consequence.

Q.   You see all three working together?

A.   Yes. If they support different proposals, then there is usually more work to do. They can also correct one another and generate more material to consider. Sometimes three are better than one.

CHAPTER FOUR

THE DEVELOPMENT
OF ARGUMENTATIVE DIALOGUES

▼

Once you have learned how to uncover the relevant observations, value judgments and assumptions of different points of view, you are ready to engage in argumentative dialogues with others.

Arguments + Dialogue = Argumentative Dialogues

Development of reasons for positions

Joint search for the meaning of things through words

A common endeavor to discover the good reasons for different positions on controversial issues.

In contrast to a debate that pits one person against another to see who wins and who loses, dialogue brings people together in a joint endeavor to increase their understanding.

Dialogue	Debate
Driven by implicit meanings	Driven by individual interests
Supports strengths	Exploits weaknesses
Strengthens community	Increases alienation
Participants explore positions	Participants protect positions
Face each other as partners	Face each other as combatants

A STORYBOARD FOR ARGUMENTATIVE DIALOGUES

Setting

A group of people have been called together to decide what they should do. The participants have different opinions about the right course of action.

Because they have different opinions, the participants also bring different resources. They gain access to them through **disagreement**. Instead of being discouraged by a scarcity of resources, they are encouraged by the potential abundance of resources for making the best decision possible.

Acknowledging their differences provides them with an opportunity for the **mutual development** of their resources.

Actors

Participants recognize one another and their organization as **moral agents**. Moral agents have the ability to recognize options, to choose one option over others, and to give reasons for the choice. In other words, persons are seen as free and as rational.

The communality of participation overrides the separateness caused by rank and hierarchy. When people do not use their rank and power to intimidate others, more lasting decisions are likely to occur. Through dialogue, participants expand their thinking beyond their previous stances and become involved in a **learning community**.

Action

Participants, engaged in **a common inquiry**, discuss the reasons for different positions. They search for resources in all positions presented, seeking to discover those that will enable them to make the best possible decision.

They **participate in the creativity of dialogue**, as they elicit from one another the implicit meanings of what they have said, and begin to discern what should be said.

When they have reached an agreement, or have run out of time without one, they **decide what should be done**.

The "tools" for the argumentative process are questions, beginning with "Why?", "So What?" and "Will it work?", and continuing with other questions that carry the dialogue forward. After posing **questions of inquiry** that seek to uncover the implicit resources, the participants ask **questions of judgment** that attempt to evaluate strengths and weaknesses.

Argumentative dialogues do not happen all at once; they entail a continual **process**, a process peppered with the pauses and interruptions you'd expect when people must make a decision. Even after a decision is made, the dialogues usually continue in response to changing conditions and new challenges.

Purpose

People become engaged in the process because they are faced with difficult controversies. One purpose of argumentative dialogues is **to make the best decision possible** given the available resources.

Another purpose is the **development of a moral community**. As participants examine different values and assumptions, and imagine the effects of their decisions on others, they also increase their awareness of the common human struggle for meaning and for justice.

MAPPING ARGUMENTATIVE DIALOGUES

In a pure dialogical process, the participants become involved in a synergistic process wherein they discover what to say. Such dialogue cannot be planned. Partners need to wait, listen, and then give voice to what they had never thought before.

Argumentative dialogues are less pure and not so open-ended. They are a response to a specific question: "What should we do?" They seek an answer.

The "map" on the next page can guide your argumentative dialogues. The process parallels the worksheets in Chapter Two. Once you have completed the map, you can use the three ethical approaches to evaluate it. Your evaluation may help you to develop a new modified proposal that includes the best resources from both views.

The map can be used:

- to develop presentations of different positions on controversial issues, showing how partners can work together to develop resources for better decisions.

- to write papers that explore the strengths and weaknesses of alternative views.

- to enter into dialogue with positions presented in articles and papers, by sorting out the implicit resources their authors used and comparing them with your own.

- to clarify the confused ramblings of many conversations.

Becoming competent in identifying the elements of argumentative dialogues and in assessing their reliability and validity does not give anyone perfect knowledge. It does, however, give everyone access to resources that we have inherited and developed, but too often over-looked or taken for granted.

QUESTION
What should we do about _____

PROPOSALS

I think we should _____

I think we should _____

"Why?"   OBSERVATIONS   "Why?"

Because _____

Because _____

"So What?"   VALUE
                    JUDGMENTS   "So What?"

So, I believe that _____

So, I believe that _____

"Will it Work?"   ASSUMPTIONS   "Will it Work?"

I assume that _____

I assume that _____

MODIFIED PROPOSAL

So, we should do it unless (or if) ___

So, we should do it unless (or if) ___

CONCLUSION

Remember the old joke about the man searching for something under a street light late at night? Someone came by and asked what he was doing. He answered that he was looking for his house keys. The passer-by asked where he had lost them. He replied he had lost them on the other side of the street. "So why not look there?" "Because," the man said, "the light is better over here."

We don't always find the resources for making good decisions on the path of least resistance. In many cases, they become available to us through acknowledging our differences and our disagreements.

The Ethical Process of decision making is a communicative practice. Its success depends on our capacity to respect our differences and our willingness to mutually explore our different "worlds."

Having dialogue with those you disagree with does not require a lack of conviction about important matters. It does require, however, that you're not so mired in a position that it becomes impossible to listen to the reasons of those who disagree with you.

The Ethical Process, which is empowered by the moral commitment to a more humane and just world, requires that people have convictions. At the same time, as people become involved in the hard work of ethical reflection, they may find themselves participating in the development of moral communities, and discover their convictions strengthened in the process.

Although the Ethical Process has been carefully outlined in this workbook, it is much more perplexing in everyday life. All the elements we have sorted out are jumbled together. Still, in many situations, awareness of the process can help us to look in the right place for the resources to make good decisions.

APPENDIX

AN EXAMPLE
OF AN ARGUMENTATIVE DIALOGUE

AN ARGUMENTATIVE DIALOGUE ON DRUG TESTING

Max   We need to decide whether we should begin a drug testing program.

Sara   Yes, and I've been thinking about this. I don't think we should.

Max   Why do you say that?

Sara   I think drug testing invades a person's privacy.

Max   How does it do that?

Sara   Well, the employer gains information about a person's private life.

Max   I agree with that. But so what?

Sara   I believe we all have privacy rights.

Max   I agree with you there too, but we need to consider other factors than privacy. I think we should do drug testing because it will decrease drug-influenced accidents and unsafe products.

Sara   I suppose it will, but I don't know how widespread drug use is.

Max   I don't know for sure either, but it seems certain that if we do not institute a drug testing program, we will have some accidents.

Sara   Well, I think we need more information before we can agree on the extent of drug use in our company. Even if drug testing increases safety, that doesn't mean we should do it.

Max   Can't we agree that management has a responsibility to maintain a safe work place?

Sara   I think we all want a safe workplace.

Max   So you agree with my argument that we should have drug testing because it will increase safety and we should maintain a safe workplace.

Sara   I agree with your reasons, but not your proposal. You seemed to agree with my reasons too.

Max   Yes, I value a person's privacy, but sometimes we have to give a little to gain a lot.

Sara   That's true, but who gives and who gains? Look, we have different observations and value judgments, but they do not contradict each other. If we are to understand the source of our disagreement, we need to look at our assumptions. You seem to assume that managers have a right to do things to employees that they would not do to themselves.

Max   Well, I wouldn't put it that way. I do assume that management has a responsibility for safety. Isn't that what management has always had?

Sara   Well, just because someone has done something does not mean they should do it. Anyway, I find your assumption intriguing. Let me ask you, "Who should be most concerned about my safety?"

Max   You should be.

Sara   Right. Doesn't it seem that employees would have a greater concern for a safe workplace than managers? After all, it is their safety we are talking about.

Max   Yes, but that assumes that workers will actually do what is best for themselves, and that what is good for employees is good for the company. With our present workforce that is a risky assumption.

Sara   Perhaps, but we are dealing with assumptions here. Remember McGregor's distinction between Theory X and Theory Y styles of management. Theory X assumes that workers want to avoid work and responsibility. Theory Y assumes that workers want to be productive and responsible. Your assumption seems more like Theory X.

Max   Perhaps we do have different approaches here. I hadn't connected management theory to the drug testing issue before. I think of myself as using a Theory Y management style, but in this case, I am not sure I trust workers to avoid drugs.

Sara   That may be one source of our disagreement.

Max   Perhaps. I am certainly not ready to disapprove of all drug testing. Although I appreciate a person's right to privacy, it seems that we talk too much about rights and not enough about responsibility. If I think about what I would have to assume to agree with you, it seems I have to assume that individuals who claim their rights will also be responsible.

Sara   I assume so.

Max   Well, that seems too individualistic to me. We need to consider a company's culture and how groups influence individual behavior. Drug testing will send a message about what kind of company we want to become and will help to shape the corporate culture. A lot of people follow the crowd. They are not the responsible individuals you imagine.

Sara   I agree that we are shaped by our society and certainly we see a rise in drug use, so I guess more individuals have followed the trend.

Max   Perhaps you cannot have responsible individuals until you have a responsible society.

Sara   Or is it the other way around?

Max   It must be some balance of the two. Drug testing could change the social trend of drug use.

Sara   Yes, and it could also decrease individual responsibility by violating individual rights.

Max   It seems like we are not going to agree on this.

Sara   I guess not, but I think we have learned about the strengths of both positions. I want you to know that I think safety is important and that I also recognize the reality of social trends.

Max   We have also discovered the need for some balance between group and individual action. I want our proposals to respect individual autonomy and basic civic rights.

Sara   Let me suggest that we refrain from drug testing because of its infringement on individual rights until and unless we observe an increase in accidents and poor productivity.

Max   Thanks for including some of my reasons in your proposal. Qualifying your position would make it easier to monitor. What about beginning with my proposal? "We should perform drug testing, unless we discover that it causes a decrease in individual self esteem and individual responsibility."

Sara   Well, you have added my basic concern, but in this case I think we should find out more information about employee attitudes toward drug testing. Since we are doing something to them, we need to listen to them first.

Max   We are supposed to decide this ourselves. Maybe that is the crux of the disagreement between us.

Sara   It is more complicated than that. We need to balance safety and privacy, and we need to find a management theory that conforms to our notions of individual responsibility and collective trends.

Max   Maybe we can understand these issues by using different ethical approaches. My arguments seem to align themselves with an ethics of consequence. When I look at the probable consequences of drug testing, the positive results seem to outweigh the negative.

Sara   How do you figure that?

Max   The positive consequence will be less risk of accidents and fewer poor quality products. The negative consequence might be that some individuals will feel we have violated their rights. At the same time, they may appreciate a safe workplace, which would be another positive consequence.

Sara   You also need to consider the long-term consequences of drug testing upon employee morale and trust. Perhaps in the long run, the overall consequences will be negative.

Max   That is difficult to measure. If we do not test, we are facing the probability of more accidents and poor products, and I don't think we can accept these consequences.

Sara   Since an analysis of all the consequences seems so difficult, perhaps our decision should be guided by an ethics of principle.

Max   Your argument seems closer to that approach.

Sara   Respecting people's right to privacy can be willed as a universal moral law, and it does treat persons as moral agents. My argument does conform to this approach.

Max   I wonder if drug testing has an implied principle that could become a moral law.

Sara   A proposal that allows one group of persons to test another group seems to set up an inequality that would be hard to universalize. If the implicit principle was that everyone should be tested for fitness, I suppose it could be universalized. This proposal, however, must also treat persons with respect to fully align itself with the principle approach.

Max   Whether we respect others with this proposal may depend more on its implementation than on the proposal itself.

Sara   Perhaps. Let's think about this from an ethics of purpose approach.

Max   The purpose of the company is to produce quality products and services. To do this we need a reliable workforce. So drug testing could be seen as a means toward achieving the company's end. The end justifies the means.

Sara   We need to consider not only what the company should do, but also what it should become. I mean we need to consider the kind of work community we should become.

Max   Well, a productive workplace should become a place where people work cooperatively together in getting the job done.

Sara   Yes, so the question is whether drug testing will promote such cooperation or not. If the cooperation requires trust, then it seems that drug testing would not, because it signals a lack of trust between the company and its workforce.

Max   It seems that the internal and external goals conflict.

Sara   That depends on your assumptions again. It seems that the three ethical approaches favor not testing. The analysis of consequences has not provided a clear cut answer. The ethics of principle seems to favor not testing because of the requirement to treat others with respect, and the ethics of purpose certainly gives as much weight to not testing as to testing. What do you think?

Max   I tend to agree. Whichever proposal we implement could turn the scales in the other direction depending on what happens in the future.

Sara   I can agree with that. We need different views to monitor any implementation so that we change our proposal if the consequences warrant it.

Max   Let's postpone the implementation of drug testing for six months. During that time we will monitor safety, and we will begin conversations with employees about their participation in ensuring a safe work place.

Sara   I agree with that. If we discover a rise in accidents or poor quality products due to drug use, then we will begin a testing program.

Max   I think we should share what we have learned with our department.

Sara   Yes. I would like the department to go through this process as well.

Max   Thanks.

Sara   And thank you.